P9-BYH-011

Measure Up!

TIME

Navin Sullivan

mc **Marshall Cavendish**
Benchmark
New York

Marshall Cavendish Benchmark
99 White Plains Road
Tarrytown, New York 10591
www.marshallcavendish.us

Text and illustrations copyright © 2007 by Marshall Cavendish Corporation
Map on page 23 by Robert Romangoli
All rights reserved. No part of this book may be reproduced or utilized in any form or by any means electronic or
mechanical including photocopying, recording, or by any information storage and retrieval system, without permission
from the copyright holders.

All Web sites were available and accurate when this book was sent to press.

Library of Congress Cataloging-in-Publication Data

Sullivan, Navin.
  Time / by Navin Sullivan.
    p. cm. — (Measure up!)
  Summary: "Discusses the time, the science behind measuring time, and the
different systems and devices used to measure time"—Provided by publisher.
  Includes bibliographical references and index.
  ISBN-13: 978-0-7614-2321-8
  ISBN-10: 0-7614-2321-4
  1. Time measurements—Juvenile literature. 2. Time
measurements—Instruments—Juvenile literature. 3. Time—Juvenile
literature. I. Title.
  QB213.S87 2007
  529'.7—dc22
  2006023231

Editor: Karen Ang
Editorial Director: Michelle Bisson
Art Director: Anahid Hamparian
Series Designer: Alex Ferrari

Photo Research by Iain Morrison

Title page caption: An Aztec calendar

Cover: Michael Rutherford/Superstock

The photographs in this book are used by permission and through the courtesy of: *Alamy:* Peter M. Wilson, 8; Ambient
Images, Inc., 28. *Envision:* Steven Mark Needham, 21. *The Image Works:* British Museum/HIP 12; AAAC/Topham: 15;
SSPL, 26, 30, 31, 34, 38; Bob Daemmrich, 42. *The Natural History Museum, London:* 37. *Photo Researchers, Inc.:*
George Holton, 1; Mehan Kulyk, 6; Jean-Loup Charmet: 13; Mike Agliolo: 18; Cordelia Molloy: 20; James King-
Holmes, 39; Peter Ryan, 41. *PictureQuest:* Antonio M. Rosario, 4; John Sanford: 10.

Printed in China
1 3 5 6 4 2

Contents

Earth spins upon an axis, bringing day and night.

CHAPTER ONE

What Is Time?

What is time? You cannot see it, you cannot touch it, yet you experience it. You know that time is passing because of all the events that happen each day.

Every morning you wake up to a new day. While you slept, Earth was silently spinning around, much like a carousel. The planet is still spinning even as you read this. As Earth turns in and out of the Sun's light, it carries you from day to night and back to day again.

The spinning Earth travels through space following an orbit—or path—around the Sun. Every year the planet travels 580 million miles. That is the length of one lap around the Sun. A year is defined as the time it takes for Earth to make one orbit around the Sun. This journey brings us the changing seasons.

Why do we have seasons? Imagine a line going right through the center of Earth from the North Pole to the South Pole. This line is Earth's axis. The planet rotates around this axis. Earth's axis is not exactly vertical, which is why an accurate globe is always displayed at a tilt. Because of this tilt, the halves of the planet get varying amounts of sunlight during different times of the year.

We divide Earth into two halves, called **hemispheres**, by an imaginary line running around the middle. This line is called the Equator.

Above the Equator is the northern hemisphere, below it is the southern hemisphere. Because of Earth's tilt, the different hemispheres get different amounts of sunlight. In midsummer and midwinter the Sun shines equally on both halves. When one half gets the most sunshine, it is summer. At that time, the other half is in winter, experiencing the least amount of sunshine. Fall and spring are between those extremes, receiving varying amounts of sunlight.

As Earth travels around the sun, it carries us into one season after another. The changing seasons were one of the first ways humans marked—or counted—time.

While one half of Earth is in the light of the Sun, the other half is in shadow.

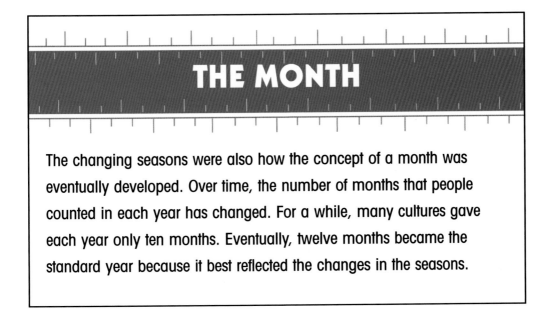

THE MONTH

The changing seasons were also how the concept of a month was eventually developed. Over time, the number of months that people counted in each year has changed. For a while, many cultures gave each year only ten months. Eventually, twelve months became the standard year because it best reflected the changes in the seasons.

MARKING A YEAR THROUGH SEASONS

Imagine you are an early Native American, living on the Great Plains long before European settlement. You would have no clocks or calendars to measure time. You would not know about the spinning Earth and its journey around the Sun. How would you mark time?

Early Native Americans—as well as other cultures around the world—noticed the changes in the environment and made sense of these changes. A day was determined from the rising and setting of the Sun. They planted and harvested food or hunted wild animals based on the changing seasons. Over time, the changing seasons indicated the passing of what was later called a year.

The change in seasons happens gradually, day by day. In the spring, the Sun travels farther north before setting, making the days longer. Eventually, the longest day of the year arrives when the Sun shines for the longest period of time. This day was eventually called the **summer solstice.** Using a modern calendar, we calculate that it occurs around June 21 or 22. After the summer solstice, the days start to become shorter. This continues until the shortest day of the year, the **winter solstice,** which occurs on December 22 or 23. After the winter solstice, the days begin lengthening again. This marks the birth of a new year.

Halfway between each solstice is one day when day and night are equal in length. This day is called an **equinox.** There are two equinoxes

El Castillo was built by the Maya. The building has a total of 365 steps representing the number of days in a solar year. Additional structures on the pyramid throw interesting shadows during the spring and fall equinoxes. When the sun sets, the shadow looks like a snake slithering down the steps of the pyramid.

every year. The spring or **vernal equinox** is on March 20 or 21. The fall or **autumnal equinox** is on September 22 or 23.

The solstices and equinoxes divide the year into four sections. Keeping track of these changes creates a calendar of sorts. People who lived in ancient times marked time using the solstices and equinoxes. They used very large stones or wooden pillars that lined up with the Sun during the solstices and equinoxes. When the Sun was lined up with these structures, they knew what time of year it was. Some of the ancient cultures that used these ancient calendars were the Celts of Europe, the Egyptians of North Africa, the Maya of Central America, and the Native Americans in North America. Many early cultures had special festivals or celebrations honoring these special times of year. Some of these celebrations are still practiced today.

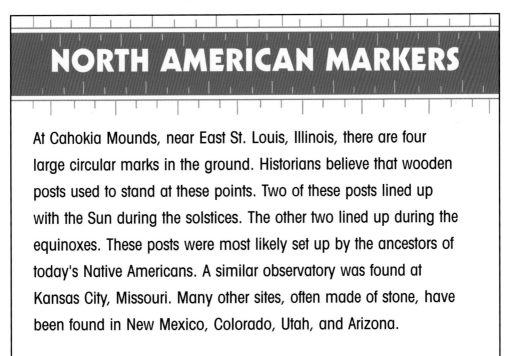

NORTH AMERICAN MARKERS

At Cahokia Mounds, near East St. Louis, Illinois, there are four large circular marks in the ground. Historians believe that wooden posts used to stand at these points. Two of these posts lined up with the Sun during the solstices. The other two lined up during the equinoxes. These posts were most likely set up by the ancestors of today's Native Americans. A similar observatory was found at Kansas City, Missouri. Many other sites, often made of stone, have been found in New Mexico, Colorado, Utah, and Arizona.

With the exception of the Sun, Sirius—the Dog Star—is the brightest star in the sky.

CHAPTER TWO

Calendars

Many early calendars were developed based on the changing seasons. Different cultures used other aspects of nature to determine how much time had passed.

THE ANCIENT EGYPTIAN CALENDAR

In Ancient Egypt about 3,000 years ago, farmers depended on the waters of the Nile River. Every summer, the Nile began flooding. According to our calendar, this happened in early July. Eventually the waters fell back to their normal level (this occurred a few months later, around September). The waters left behind rich new soil that had been carried downstream. This soil was good for crops, and the farmers would do their planting at this time. The crops would be ready for harvesting in the spring (around April).

To plan for these events, the farmers needed a calendar. They noticed that the flood occurred about every 365 days, so they made that their year. Unfortunately, 365 days is a little less than a year. By sticking to their calendar, the farmers were planting their crops earlier and earlier. Over a few years, that made no real difference, but over centuries it mattered a lot. Crops were no longer being planted at the right time.

To correct this, the Egyptians turned to their astronomers for help with measuring the year exactly.

The astronomers found a way of defining the year using the stars instead of the Sun. As Earth orbits the Sun, we can see the constellations—or arrangements of stars—from different angles. One star, Sirius—called the Dog Star—is only visible 290 days a year. The astronomers saw Sirius first appear each year when the Nile's floods began. The next year Sirius first appeared 364 1/4 days later. This, then, gave them the true length of the year. Since it is inconvenient to count a quarter of a day, they suggested adding one extra day to the calendar every fourth year. This would change the calendar, and help the people count the passing time correctly. However, Egypt's rulers refused to alter the official calendar. So Egypt's farmers made up for the faulty calendar by adding an extra day or so to their unofficial calendar from time to time. The extra day was officially added about 3,000 years later, when the Ancient Romans changed the calendar.

An Ancient Egyptian calendar uses hieroglyphs to keep track of certain days of the year.

LUNAR CALENDAR

Because the Moon circles Earth about once a month, the year was defined as twelve cycles of the Moon. This is the lunar year. (Lunar refers to the Moon.) However, the Moon orbits Earth every 29 1/2 days, so a lunar year is only 354 days. This is 11 1/4 days less than the time it takes for Earth to orbit the Sun. It is likely that the lunar calendar was developed, used, and changed by the Ancient Babylonians, the Ancient Greeks, and the Ancient Romans.

Lunar calendars are no longer considered accurate for everyday use. But many religious festivals were—and still are—tied to the different phases of the Moon. Christian, Jewish, Muslim, and other religious calendars still incorporate lunar cycles. For example, the Jewish Passover begins on the first full moon following the spring equinox. Christians celebrate Easter Sunday on the first Sunday after the first full moon that follows the spring equinox.

Different parts of this French lunar calendar from 1680 can be moved to keep track of days in the lunar cycles.

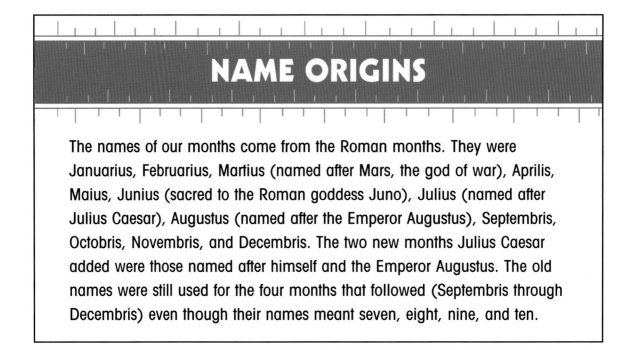

NAME ORIGINS

The names of our months come from the Roman months. They were Januarius, Februarius, Martius (named after Mars, the god of war), Aprilis, Maius, Junius (sacred to the Roman goddess Juno), Julius (named after Julius Caesar), Augustus (named after the Emperor Augustus), Septembris, Octobris, Novembris, and Decembris. The two new months Julius Caesar added were those named after himself and the Emperor Augustus. The old names were still used for the four months that followed (Septembris through Decembris) even though their names meant seven, eight, nine, and ten.

SOLAR CALENDAR

The solar calendar is based on the time it takes Earth to orbit the Sun, which is about 365 days each year. The Ancient Romans started with ten calendar months in a year. These months were longer than the months we use today, but they did not reflect the seasons very well. The Romans eventually added two more months and made each of them more or less equal in length to fit the solar year. Our present months were devised by the Ancient Romans during the reign of Julius Caesar around 46 BCE. This twelve-month calendar is often called the Julian Calendar or the Old Style Calendar.

Pegs were used to mark months, days, and years on this Roman calendar.

The Romans also added an extra day every fourth year, just as the Ancient Egyptian astronomers had wanted long before. These years are called **leap years.** Today we pretty much follow the Roman solar calendar and take leap years into account. Our basic year is 365 days, but every fourth year we add an extra day at the end of February. Nearly all of the months are thirty or thirty-one days. The exception is February, which has twenty-eight days during a regular year and twenty-nine during a leap year.

USEFUL RHYMES

An old Quaker rhyme from Pennsylvania was used to help people memorize the days of the months:

Fourth, eleventh, ninth, and sixth
Thirty days to each affix
Every other thirty-one
Except the second month alone.

You might be more familiar with this old nursery rhyme:

Thirty days hath September,
April, June, and November,
All the rest have thirty-one,
Excepting February alone,
Which has but twenty-eight days clear
And twenty-nine in each leap year.

GREGORIAN CALENDAR

Over time, the Roman calendar turned out to be inadequate. The leap year adjustment was a little too much. Approximately 1,000 years after Julius Caesar, six days had been added to the year. By 1582 it was even worse—a year was ten days too long!

The Roman Catholic pope at that time, Gregory XIII, decided to change the calendar. This new calendar was called the Gregorian calendar. The Gregorian year begins in January. Leap years still occurred about every four years. But in order for a leap year to begin a century, its number had to be divisible by 400. For example, the years 1600 and 2000 were leap years because the 1,600 and 2,000 are evenly divisible by 400. But the years 1700 and 1900 were not leap years. This reduced the calendar error so that the calendar would only be wrong by one day every 3,300 years. Pope Gregory XIII also canceled the ten extra days that had accumulated from the errors in the Roman calendar. His decision took effect on October 4, 1582, and the next day became October 15! When Pope Gregory XIII canceled ten days in 1582, many people were unhappy. They thought that he had taken away ten days from their lives. Many pleaded: "Give us back our ten days!"

Eventually, nearly all the nations in the world adopted the Gregorian calendar. Sometimes the Gregorian calendar is called the New Style Calendar.

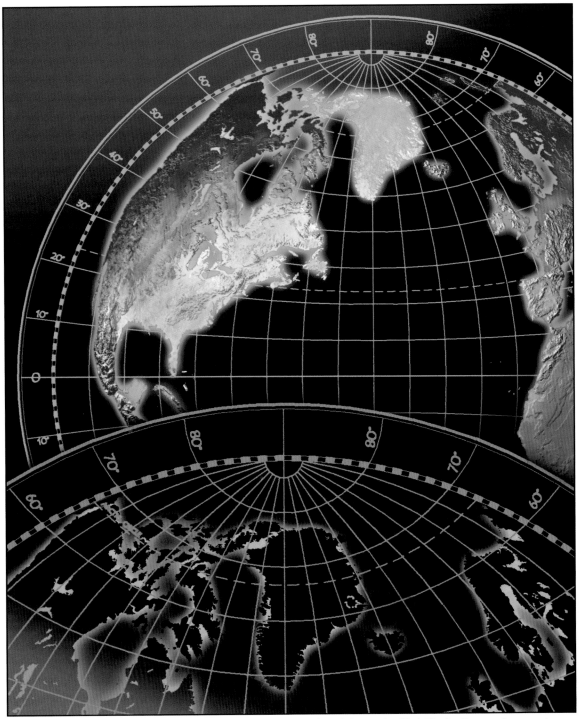

Longitude helps determine the time around the world, but when it is used with latitude, it can give exact locations of places.

CHAPTER THREE

The Day

As Earth orbits the Sun, the planet is spinning on its axis in a **counterclockwise** direction. The Sun only shines on one half of the planet at a time, leaving the other half in shadow. When you are having breakfast, people on the other side of the world are going to bed. The time it takes for Earth to spin once around its axis—twenty-four hours—is one day.

LONGITUDE

To know what the time is in different parts of the world, we divide the planet up with twenty-four imaginary lines—one for each hour of the day. These lines run north to south from pole to pole around Earth in a set of vertical circles. They are called lines of longitude, or meridians. Travel east to west across twelve of these lines, and you have gone halfway around the world.

The time between any two lines of longitude is always one hour, but the lines of longitude are not always the same distance apart from each other. This is because Earth is a sphere. The distance around the planet is smaller toward the poles, and greatest at the Equator.

Hours are represented by longitude, but where do we begin counting? In 1884 an international conference decided to start at Greenwich, England. This was because at that time, Greenwich was the site of the world's premier astronomical observatory. The longitude that traveled through Greenwich was called the zero meridian or the **prime meridian.**

The prime meridian is marked as it passes through the Greenwich Observatory.

Lines of longitude are labeled in degrees. Each meridian is separated by 15 degrees. The prime meridian is 0 degrees (0°). If you traveled west of the prime meridian, the next line of longitude is 15° West (15° W). Two lines of longitude east of the prime meridian is 30° East (30° E). There are eleven meridians east of the prime meridian and eleven west. The meridian at 180°—which is neither East nor West—is opposite from the Greenwich Meridian. This line is called the **international date line.**

One way to understand how the lines of longitude splay out from the poles involves looking at an orange. You will need an orange and a ruler. Carefully take off the peel of the orange, making sure to keep the fruit whole.

Using the ruler, notice how each segment is wider toward the middle than at the top or bottom of the orange. This is similar to longitudinal lines that stretch around the planet.

The segments of an orange are similar to the segments of Earth when the planet is divided by meridians.

WHERE DOES EACH DAY BEGIN?

The day's twenty-four hours are counted from Greenwich, but the day does not start there. Instead, the day begins at the international date line.

On either side of the date line the time is the same, but the day is different. Cross the international date line from east to west and you move into the day before. If it is Wednesday east of the date line, then it is Tuesday west of the line. Travel across the line from west to east and you move into the next day. Will you be a different age? Yes, but only by a day, and that will not affect how long you live!

TIME ZONES

The meridians divide Earth into twenty-four time zones. The time at the Greenwich Meridian is called **Greenwich Mean Time (GMT).** To figure out the time east of Greenwich is GMT plus the number of meridians from Greenwich. So the time difference between Greenwich and a city that is two meridians away is two hours. If it is 3 o'clock in Greenwich, then it will be 5 o'clock in an eastern city that is two meridians away. To the west, the time is GMT minus the number of meridians, or in this case, 1 o'clock.

The areas covered by time zones do not follow the longitudinal lines exactly. Though the meridians are straight lines, the borders of time zones are not necessarily straight lines. For example, the international date line actually runs around Kiribati, an island nation in the Pacific Ocean.

The United States and its territories cover so much space that they use eight of the world's twenty-four time zones. The easternmost time zone is the Atlantic Standard Time zone (AST). This includes Puerto Rico and the U.S. Virgin Islands. Moving west from there are the following zones: Eastern Standard Time (EST), Central Standard Time (CST), Mountain Standard Time (MST), Pacific Standard Time (PST), Alaskan Standard Time (AKST), Hawaiian-Aleutian Standard Time (HST), and Samoa Standard Time (UTC-11). The Samoa Standard Time Zone includes American Samoa, a United States territory in the South Pacific Ocean.

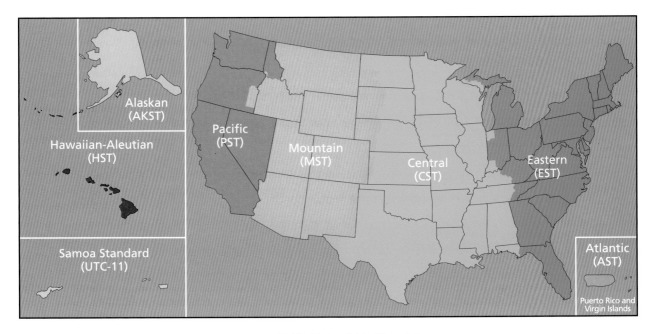

The United States and its territories are divided into eight different time zones.

Usually, several states make up a time zone. Some time zones actually cross through and divide several states, such as Nebraska, North Dakota, and South Dakota, to name a few. This means that there will be a time difference between different parts of these states. Hawaii is the only state to have its own time zone.

Eastern Standard Time is GMT minus five hours. Can you figure out what time it is in the other American time zones?

DAYLIGHT SAVING TIME

Daylight Saving Time is a system that was developed so that daytime hours would fall when there was daylight. This was especially ideal during times of war, when a nation needed to use less electricity or fuel to provide light for its workers. If the daytime hours (which was the time when most people worked) matched the time the sun was out, then less money and energy was spent lighting factories and other businesses.

For many years—in most of the United States—Daylight Saving Time was applied by adding one hour to the clocks at 2:00 a.m. on the first Sunday in April. One hour was taken away at 2:00 a.m. on the last Sunday in October. After 2007, one hour is added on the second Sunday in March instead of in April. The hour is be subtracted on the first Sunday in November. This change in schedule was made in order to help conservation efforts to save energy and protect the environment and the planet's natural resources.

Other countries practice Daylight Saving Time at slightly different times of the year—or not at all.

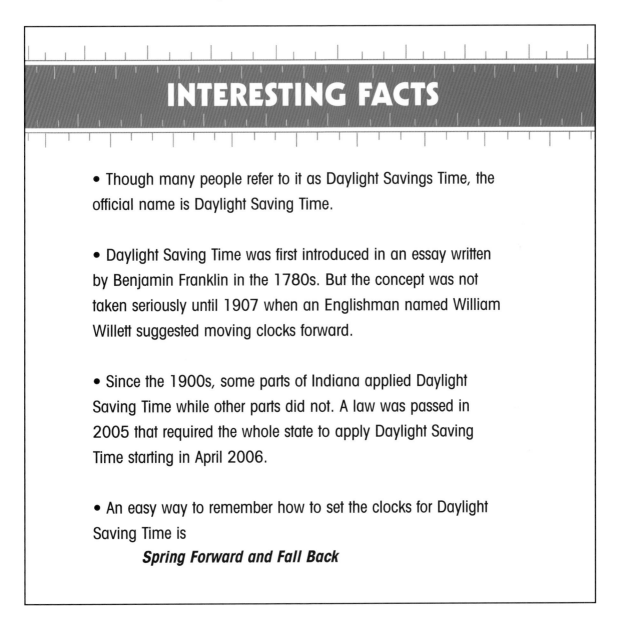

INTERESTING FACTS

• Though many people refer to it as Daylight Savings Time, the official name is Daylight Saving Time.

• Daylight Saving Time was first introduced in an essay written by Benjamin Franklin in the 1780s. But the concept was not taken seriously until 1907 when an Englishman named William Willett suggested moving clocks forward.

• Since the 1900s, some parts of Indiana applied Daylight Saving Time while other parts did not. A law was passed in 2005 that required the whole state to apply Daylight Saving Time starting in April 2006.

• An easy way to remember how to set the clocks for Daylight Saving Time is
Spring Forward and Fall Back

The Wells Cathedral clock was made in the 1390s and was one of the early mechanical clocks. Today, it is the third-oldest surviving mechanical clock in the world.

CHAPTER FOUR
Measuring Time

Throughout history, humans have looked for ways to measure time. Today we use clocks and watches. The kind of clock we use depends upon our purposes. For example, if you are baking a pie, you need an oven clock that registers minutes. If the clock only told time in hours your food would be ruined. Similarly, the clocks on VCR-s or DVD recorders need to register time in seconds so that you will not miss the start of your favorite show or movie. Activities that are timed in fractions of seconds require even more specialized clocks. Professional races are timed with clocks that register to 1/100 second.

A clock that registers time in smaller divisions will be more accurate in its measurements. (Similarly, using a ruler that is divided into fractions of an inch is more accurate than using a ruler that measures only inches.) In their quest for accuracy, humans have developed even more exact clocks. It is now possible to measure time to one billionth of a second!

THE FIRST CLOCKS

In 1500 BCE the Ancient Egyptians invented hours. They split daytime into twelve equal parts. They did not split the nighttime. Summer days have more daylight than winter days, so they made their summer hours longer, too.

The Ancient Egyptians used sunlight and shadow to measure time. In sunlight a vertical stick throws a shadow. When the Sun is low in the sky, in morning or evening, the shadow is long. As the Sun climbs across the sky, the shadow shortens. The shadow is shortest in the middle of the day. People often refer to this time as high noon.

The Egyptians used the positions of the shadow throughout the day to make a clock. Noon became the time when the shortest shadow was displayed. They divided the remaining shadow positions into twelve equal hours—six on each side. These were the earliest sundials. For important clocks used in public places, the sticks were replaced with tapering stone pillars called obelisks. In the nineteenth century some of the great Egyptian obelisks were transported to other countries. Those in London and New York are known as Cleopatra's Needles.

This obelisk is in New York's Central Park.

WATER CLOCKS

Later, Ancient Egyptians wanted to measure time at night as well as in daytime. They could not use sunlight to measure the hours at night, so they created a water clock. With this clock they were able to divide both daytime and nighttime into hours, and ended up with a day of twenty-four hours.

The water clock was a stone bowl with a hole at the bottom. The bowl was filled with water. As the water trickled out, its falling level indicated the passing of time. How fast the water flowed out depended on the shape of the bowl, the size of the hole, and the height of water remaining in the bowl. With a straight-sided bowl, the water level decreased slowly, the flow through the hole slowed down, and time seemed to be going by more slowly. This was not an accurate way to tell time, so the Ancient Egyptians made the bowl conical or cone-shaped. The bowl became narrower from top to bottom. This kept the water from losing height too quickly and evened out the rate at which the water flowed out through the hole. Inside the bowl, levels were marked to show the changes in water level each hour. Other cultures also developed such water clocks.

About a century after the Ancient Egyptians invented their water clocks, the Chinese developed an even better water clock. A vertical wheel carried twenty-four small cups around its rim. Water was poured into the first cup. The cup was filled in one hour. The weight of the cup and water was then just enough to make the cup fall. When the cup fell, the wheel turned, marking the passing of an hour. As the wheel turned, it brought down the next cup to be filled. A glance at the number of cups that had been filled revealed how many hours had gone by. By 1300 CE, Chinese water clocks were keeping such good time that in each twenty-four hours they were accurate to thirty seconds. This meant that the time kept by the water clocks was only off by about thirty seconds a day—an impressive accomplishment.

But the water clock had a few drawbacks. Just as a sundial needs the Sun, a water clock needs water. What would happen in a cold climate where the water freezes? Or a very hot climate where the water would evaporate quickly?

This is a working model of a Chinese water clock used around 1088.

SAND CLOCKS

To get around the lack of sunlight and freezing water, people tried clocks that used sand. A sand clock had an upper and lower chamber, connected by a thin neck. Sand from the upper chamber fell steadily into the bottom chamber. The width of the neck and the amount of sand left in the upper chamber controlled the rate at which the sand fell. In some of the first sand clocks, the falling level of sand in the upper chamber indicated the passing of the hours. Sand clocks that measure one hour are called hourglasses. By using different-sized sand clocks people could measure different amounts of time.

Unfortunately, measuring a long time required a lot of sand. Additionally, the clock needed to be turned upside down once the upper chamber was empty. That would be very difficult with all that glass and sand. As a result, big sand clocks were not popular. However, smaller sand clocks were used to mark short amounts of time. Today, small sand clocks are still used as egg timers and in some board games.

Each of these sand clocks from the eighteenth century measured a specific length of time.

MEASURING SPEED

The hourglass was used on ships to help measure their speed. A heavy log tied to the end of a 900-foot rope was thrown overboard into the water. The rope had knots tied at regular intervals or spaces. As the ship sailed on, the log stayed where it was in the water and pulled more rope out from the ship. The number of knots passing overboard per hour—with the hour measured by an hourglass— gave the ship's speed. Ships today use more sophisticated tools for measuring speed, but the speed is still quoted in knots.

THE FIRST MECHANICAL CLOCKS

To avoid problems associated with sunlight, freezing water, and heavy sand, mechanical clocks were invented. The earliest were built in southern Europe in the fourteenth century. A weight pulled a cord down and turned a wooden cylinder. The cylinder turned a clock hand around a twenty-four-hour dial. This was the first **analog clock.** The word *analog*—or analogous—is used when something is similar to something else. The hand that turned once around the clock's dial in twenty-four hours was an analog of Earth turning around its axis once in twenty-four hours. Today, analog clocks are clocks that display time using hands that move around a dial.

These early mechanical clocks had to be constantly rewound by cranking the wooden cylinder back to its original position. Doing this interrupted the working of the clock for a minute or so. Even though these clocks were simple, they were accurate enough that they only lost about fifteen minutes each twenty-four hours. Soon many churches in Europe had such clocks mounted in clock towers to signal religious services. Ordinary townsfolk, who had no clocks of their own, used the church clocks to tell the time.

PENDULUM CLOCKS

In the 1580s an Italian scientist, Galileo Galilei, watched a heavy cathedral lamp swinging on a long chain. As he watched it, the lamp swung more and more slowly, and the distance the chain swung became shorter. Galileo timed the swings using his heartbeats. He found—to his surprise—that each swing lasted the same time as the last, even though the distance was shorter. Galileo realized that this could be used to measure time. He saw that any freely swinging weight would behave the same way. This freely swinging weight is called a pendulum. Once it is started with the first swing, a pendulum keeps swinging back and forth because of the pull of Earth's gravity. The length of the swings do, however, become smaller. So the pendulum would need reinforcing from time to time to keep the swings from becoming too small.

Although Galileo thought about how a pendulum clock could be constructed, the first pendulum clock was made in Holland by Christian Huygens in 1656. It kept time accurately enough so that its time was only around ten seconds off during a twenty-four-hour period.

SPRING-CONTROLLED CLOCKS

This model of Galileo's pendulum clock was made in the nineteenth century.

In 1660 the English scientist Robert Hooke thought of powering a clock by using an uncoiling spring. As the spring uncoiled, parts of the clock would move and measure the passage of time. Of course, the spring would have to be rewound periodically. However, Hooke never made his spring-controlled clock. Christian Huygens, the inventor of the pendulum clock, made the first spring-controlled clock in 1675.

CHRONOMETERS

To know where they were on the ocean, sailors had to know their longitude. This could be calculated from the difference between the local time (where they were at that point) and the time back in their original harbor. Each hour represented 15 degrees of longitude. So the time difference gave their distance east or west of the harbor. But how could they know what the time was back in their harbor?

To measure local time, they used the Sun's position each day. For them, the day began when the Sun rose above the horizon. The Sun then moves across the sky at 15 degrees an hour. Measuring the Sun's height in degrees above the horizon gave them local time. For shore time, they needed a clock that was set when they left the harbor, and continued to tick away, keeping harbor time.

To make a truly accurate clock was a great challenge. A sailing ship pitches and rolls, so a pendulum clock was inadequate. The clock also had to withstand climatic changes in heat, air humidity, and air pressure. A clock capable of great accuracy in spite of all these factors is known as a chronometer.

In 1713 the British government offered a large prize for a reliable chronometer. An Englishman, John Harrison, rose to the challenge. His spring-controlled clock used different metals to cancel out temperature changes. In 1762, on a five-month voyage from England to Jamaica, it gained only 1/3 of a second per day! King George III awarded Harrison the prize in 1773.

SPRING-CONTROLLED WATCHES

In the 1840s the railroads spread westward across America. Every train conductor had to know the local time as he traveled. The time for each station along the route was calculated at Harvard College Observatory in Massachusetts. The time was sent to each station using the telegraph. To keep track of time between the stations, the conductor needed a wind-up watch. Such watches were called fob watches because they were attached to a chain, or fob, that was anchored to a vest pocket. In Waltham, Massachusetts, the American Waltham Watch Company became the nation's center for making fob watches. It was mass producing them for the railroads throughout the 1800s.

BATTERY AND QUARTZ CLOCKS

Pendulum and spring clocks are accurate enough for many situations. But to measure time even more accurately, you need a clock that measures fractions of a second. The quartz-crystal clock—invented in 1928 by Warren A. Marrison at Bell Laboratories in New York—does just that. An electric current from a battery makes crystals of a mineral called quartz vibrate. (To picture these vibrations, think of the vibrations of a bell that has just been struck.) Because these vibrations are very rapid, Marrison used them to measure time in 1/1000 of a second.

In 1971, Peter Dimitroff Petroff made a portable quartz watch powered by a battery. This watch was a **digital clock** that displayed the time in numbers instead of using hands and a dial. Today, whether they are digital or analog, most wristwatches use quartz crystals and batteries.

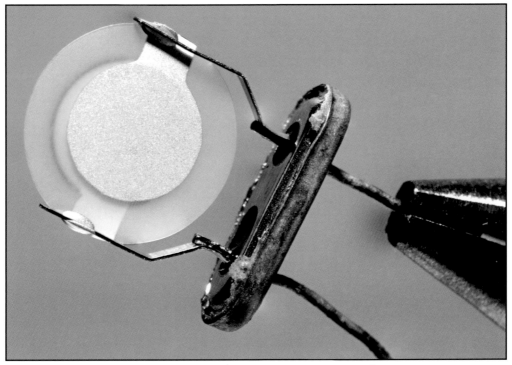

Tiny quartz crystals are used in watches and clocks to keep accurate time.

THE ATOMIC CLOCK

The cesium atomic clock is even more accurate than the quartz crystal clock. Cesium is usually a solid metal. When used in clocks, it is heated until it becomes a gas. All matter is made up of small particles called **atoms.** The atoms in the cesium gas are vibrating at a faster rate than the vibrations of a quartz crystal. The cesium atoms vibrate at a rate of more than nine billion vibrations per second. Cesium clocks can measure time to a thousand-millionth of a second. A cesium clock is calculated to be accurate to 1 second in 10 million years. Because they measure time through atomic vibrations, cesium clocks are called atomic clocks.

The first cesium atomic clock was developed in 1955.

The National Institute of Standards and Technology at Gaithersburg, Maryland, sends time signals from its cesium clock all around the world by radio, telephone, and the Internet. Airlines, banks, and internet servers can all check the exact time from its clock.

CALCULATING AGE WITHOUT CLOCKS

Sometimes even clocks cannot help us measure the amount of time that has passed. This is especially true when we try to calculate the age of something extremely old or something that people have not observed. For example, how would you find out how old an ancient artifact is? Or how would you determine the age of some trees in a forest?

CARBON DATING

Carbon is a chemical element that is present in all living things. All carbon contains two kinds of atom—regular and radioactive. The radioactive carbon atoms release different kinds of **radiation.** As they do this, they change into regular atoms. The rate of this change is constant per year. So the amount of radioactivity in carbon indicates the carbon's age. New carbon is more radioactive than old carbon.

Because living things are constantly taking in carbon, the organism's amount of radioactive carbon compared to its regular carbon remains the same. However, after the organism dies, its radioactive

A scientist prepares bone samples for radiocarbon dating.

carbon continues to decay or break down. The radioactive carbon becomes a smaller part—or proportion—of all the carbon in the organism's remains. From this proportion scientists can determine the age of the remains. This is called carbon dating or radiocarbon dating. Anything that contains carbon, such as fossilized sea creatures or pre-historic wood structures, can be carbon dated. Archaeologists—scientists who study historical artifacts—can use carbon dating to determine the age of Egyptian mummies preserved for over 3,000 years. Geologists who study the structure and processes of Earth can use carbon dating to check the age of different levels of Earth's crust if there is some carbon in the crust samples.

TREE RINGS

In the Muir Woods, north of San Francisco, there are giant redwood trees up to 2,000 years old. Many trees have been growing in their forests long before humans ever settled the land around them. But how can you determine the age of a tree that was not planted by or observed by people?

Certain types of trees add layers to their trunks as they grow each year. These layers can be seen as rings inside the trunk. The rings are visible when the tree is cut down or if its stump is left in the ground. However, there are other ways to view the growth rings without cutting down or killing the tree. Some scientists insert a hollow tube through the bark and into the center of the tree. When the tube

The freshly cut trunks of these pine trees can help determine the age of the trees and the approximate age of the forest.

is pulled out and emptied, the scientist can view the sample from the tree's center.

The inner rings are the oldest growth and the outer rings are the newest growth. Each ring counts as a year. By counting the rings scientists can figure out how old the tree is. The rings can also tell them what the climate and growing conditions were like during the different years. If it was a wet year and conditions were good for the tree, the ring would be wide. A narrow ring means it was a dry year or something happened that restricted the tree's growth. If the sample has a hollow spot or there is charcoal in the rings, the tree was probably affected by fire.

Though most people need alarm clocks to help them wake up, all humans have inner clocks that help our bodies function.

CHAPTER FIVE
Living Clocks

Travel to another time zone and what happens? You wake up too early, or you want your breakfast at midnight. Your natural inner clock has not reset itself to the new time zone, and you are still tuned in to the old time zone.

Your inner clock is actually made of many clocks. The master clock is in your brain. It is geared to a twenty-four-hour cycle. Why twenty-four hours? That is Earth's daily rotation time. We belong to Earth and our bodies are naturally attuned to it.

Your master clock is reset by daylight. Fly from New York to Los Angeles, and the daylight seems too intense because the Sun is too high in the sky. You are still accustomed to Eastern Standard Time where, at that moment, the Sun is lower in the sky. For the first couple of days you may be very tired because of the time difference. Many people call this tiredness jet lag.

But over two or three days, your body becomes accustomed to the new daylight schedule. Your eyes respond to the different daylight hours and your inner clock resets itself naturally. You know when you have adjusted because you want to go to bed and wake up at the same time as others around you.

There are clocks in other parts of your body, too. They control your muscles, organs, and other body parts involved in making your body work. When you feel sleepy, your inner clocks are winding down. Your body knows that it is time to rest and recharge. Though your inner clocks are telling you it is time to rest, they still work even while you are asleep. Your body is going through different cycles that control things such as how deeply you sleep and even when you dream. When you wake up in the morning, your clocks—and hopefully your body—are all set for the day ahead.

Besides your twenty-four-hour clock, other clocks in your body function through the years to manage your growth and development. These clocks control things such as when you lose your baby teeth and when your permanent teeth come in. The rate at which you grow also depends on these clocks.

Animals—besides humans—have inner clocks, too. A bird's inner clock tells it when to migrate. Many animals' inner clocks help them hibernate during the winter. Even insects have clocks. All these clocks seem to work in a similar way to ours.

Every plant has a biological clock that responds to temperature and exposure to light. The clocks are "programmed" so that the plants begin growing at the right time of the year. After the stem begins to grow, and the plants break into leaf or flower, the growth rate depends on the outside temperature. If the weather is warm, most plants will grow faster and bloom earlier.

MONARCH MIGRATION

Early each fall in the northern United States, millions of Monarchs hatch as caterpillars, that eventually turn into butterflies. As the weather cools, each butterfly flies 2,000 miles to Mexico, where it spends the winter. The butterflies go to oyamel trees in mountains that they have never been to before. Somehow they know to go to these trees. The trees are the ones from which their great great grandparents flew north. A built-in system in their bodies tells them to do this.

To make the flight, the butterflies need to know which direction is due south. They use the position of the Sun to find their direction. At noon, the Sun is due south, but during the rest of the day the butterflies have to correct for the Sun's movement across the sky. To do this, they use an inner clock that calculates where the Sun would be if the time was noon.

Throughout history, people have searched for ways to understand time. Thousands of years ago, the earliest men and women tried to explain time, and especially to measure it, by watching the changes in their surroundings. We do the same today, using some of the most advanced technology ever created. Why? Because we know something that our long-ago ancestors also knew—that if we do not understand time, we cannot understand our world.

GLOSSARY

analog clock—A clock that uses moving hands on a dial to show minutes, hours, or seconds.

atoms—Small particles that are known as the building blocks of all matter. All matter is made of atoms.

autumnal equinox—An equinox occurring September 22 or 23. It is also called the fall equinox.

carbon dating—A process used to determine the age of carbon-containing substances.

counterclockwise—Movement in a direction opposite from the way hands on a clock normally move.

digital clock—A clock that uses numbers to display time instead of hands on a dial.

equinox—A day halfway between each solstice when day and night are equal in length.

Greenwich Mean Time (GMT)—The time at the Greenwich Meridian. It is used to determine time in other time zones.

hemisphere—Half of a sphere. Earth's hemispheres determined using the Equator or a chosen line of longitude.

international date line—The line of longitude at 180° where day officially begins.

leap year—A year that has an extra day in February, occurring about once every four years.

longitude—Lines that divide Earth vertically from pole to pole. They are measured in degrees East or West starting from the prime meridian (0°).

prime meridian—The line of longitude passing through Greenwich, England. Its location is 0° longitude and is also called the zero meridian.

radiation—Energy released in the form of invisible rays.

summer solstice—The longest day of the year, which occurs on June 21 or 22.

vernal equinox—An equinox occurring on March 20 or 21. It is also called the spring equinox.

winter solstice—The shortest day of the year, which occurs on December 22 or 23.

FIND OUT MORE

BOOKS

Duffy, Trent. *Turning Point Inventions: The Clock.* New York: Atheneum, 2003.

Farndon, John. *Time.* New York: Benchmark Books, 2003.

Formichelli, Linda and W. Eric Martin. *Tools of Timekeeping: A Kid's Guide to the History & Science of Telling Time.* Vermont: Nomad Press, 2005.

WEB SITES

Daylight Saving Time
http://webexhibits.org/daylightsaving/c.html

The Official U.S. Time
http://www.time.gov

A Walk Through Time: The Evolution of Time Measurement through the Ages
http://physics.nist.gov/GenInt/Time/time.html

INDEX

PAGES NUMBERS FOR ILLUSTRATIONS ARE IN **BOLDFACE**

ABOUT THE AUTHOR

Navin Sullivan has an M.A. in science from the University of Cambridge. He lives with his wife in London, England, and has dedicated many years to science education. He has edited various science texts, and has written science books for younger readers. Navin Sullivan has also been the CEO of a British educational publisher and Chairman of its Boston subsidiary. His hobbies include playing the piano and chess.

529
SUL

NEW6003

Sullivan, Navin.

Time